Little Pebble™

MIGHTY
MILITARY MACHINES

Aircraft
Carriers

A 4D BOOK

by Matt Scheff

PEBBLE
a capstone imprint

Download the Capstone 4D app!

- Ask an adult to download the Capstone 4D app.
- Scan the cover and stars inside the book for additional content.

When you scan a spread, you'll find fun extra stuff to go with this book! You can also find these things on the web at www.capstone4D.com using the password: aircraftcarriers.01136

Little Pebble is published by Pebble
1710 Roe Crest Drive, North Mankato,
Minnesota 56003
www.mycapstone.com

Library of Congress Cataloging-in-Publication Data
Names: Scheff, Matt, author.
Title: Aircraft carriers : a 4D book / by Matt Scheff.
Description: North Mankato, Minnesota : Pebble, [2018] |
Series: Little pebble. Mighty military machines |
Audience: Ages 4–8.
Identifiers: LCCN 2018004136 (print) |
LCCN 2018006808 (ebook) |
ISBN 9781977101259 (eBook PDF) |
ISBN 9781977101136 (hardcover) |
ISBN 9781977101198 (paperback)
Subjects: LCSH: Aircraft carriers—Juvenile literature.
Classification: LCC V874 (ebook) |
LCC V874 .S35 2018 (print) | DDC 623.825/5—dc23
LC record available at https://lccn.loc.gov/2018004136

Editorial Credits
Marissa Kirkman, editor; Heidi Thompson, designer;
Jo Miller, media researcher; Tori Abraham, production
specialist

Photo Credits
U.S. Navy Photo by MC2 Paul L. Archer, 9, MC3 Anthony
J. Rivera, 7, MC3 Ignacio D. Perez, 11, MCSN Erika Kugler,
15, Casey J. Hopkins, cover; Wikimedia: U. S. Navy photo by
MCSN Brandon Morris, 17, MC3 Anderson W. Branch, 21,
MC3 Justin M. Smelley, 19, MCSA Rachel N. Clayton, 13,
MCSN Lauren Booher, 5
Design Elements: Shutterstock: Zerbor

Printed and bound in China.
000309

Table of Contents

Big Ships

Look! A plane is landing.

It is on an aircraft carrier.

A carrier is a navy ship.

It is big.

It carries planes.

At Sea

The ship is at sea.

It is like an airport.

Pilots fly the planes.

The crew fixes them.

pilot

crew

11

The planes take off.

They land.

Parts

This is the hull.

It is the ship's body.

It is made of steel.

hull

Engines power the ship.

They make it go.

The flight deck is big.

It is flat.

Planes land on it.

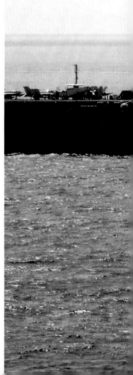

Boom! Blast!

The ship has guns.

Glossary

airport—a place where aircraft take off and land

crew—a team of people who work together

engine—a machine that makes the power needed to move something

flight deck—the long, flat area on top of an aircraft carrier where planes can take off and land

hull—the main body of a boat or ship

navy—the branch of the military that fights on water

steel—a strong type of metal

Read More

Boothroyd, Jennifer. *Inside the US Navy.* U.S. Armed Forces. Minneapolis: Lerner Publications, 2017.

Reed, Jennifer. *The U.S. Navy.* The U.S. Military Branches. North Mankato, Minn.: Capstone Press, 2018.

Willis, John. *Aircraft Carriers.* Mighty Military Machines. New York: AV2 by Weigl, 2017.

Internet Sites

Use FactHound to find Internet sites related to this book.

Visit *www.facthound.com*
Just type in 9781977101136 and go.

Super-cool stuff!
Check out projects, games and lots more at
www.capstonekids.com

Critical Thinking Questions

1. Where do airplanes land on an aircraft carrier?

2. What is the hull made of?

3. Which part gives an aircraft carrier its power?

Index